"Dawn Macdonald's poetry is alive with curiosity and truth. She speaks in conversation at times soft and at times bitter, creating images from a reality that can be obscure yet familiar. Macdonald's singular work reveals the unromantic beauty of a storied northern world full of lichen, kingfishers, and dog hair. Her poems open new paths in poetry from the high latitudes. This work is a bright addition to any library."

—ERNESTINE HAYES, Alaska State Writer Laureate 2017–2018

"In *Northerny*, Dawn Macdonald tempers a poetic soulfulness with a comic's sense for absurdity and punch. These poems speak with smart humor and wit, linguistic delight, and honest observations spiked with confession, always with an ear, too, for what their poet can't say. Macdonald's take on born-and-raised life in the north avoids romantic quagmires with a well-cured settler colonial self-consciousness. Macdonald resists worn expectations in this fresh expansion of northern literature rich with voice, earned insight, and meaning."

—JEREMY PATAKY, author of *Overwinter*

"*Northerny* echolocates around the rural, urban, and more-than-human worlds with unflinching curiousity. Macdonald's poetry bewilders language, making it romp, flit, and twist. Her images are in turn luminous and jarring cut with knife-sharp wit, unafraid to trespass against our expectations."

—CLEA ROBERTS, author of *Auguries*

NORTHERNY

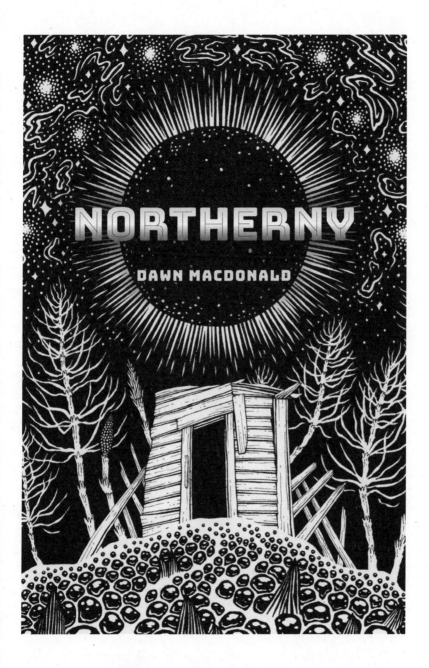

NORTHERNY

DAWN MACDONALD

 UNIVERSITY *of* **ALBERTA** PRESS

Published by

University of Alberta Press
1-16 Rutherford Library South
11204 89 Avenue NW
Edmonton, Alberta, Canada T6G 2J4
amiskwaciwâskahikan | Treaty 6 |
Métis Territory
uap.ualberta.ca | uapress@ualberta.ca

**Library and Archives Canada
Cataloguing in Publication**

Title: Northerny / Dawn Macdonald.
Names: Macdonald, Dawn (Poet), author.
Series: Robert Kroetsch series.
Description: Series statement: Robert
    Kroetsch series | Poems.
Identifiers: Canadiana (print) 20230553753 |
    Canadiana (ebook) 20230553761 |
    ISBN 9781772127379 (softcover) |
    ISBN 9781772127546 (EPUB) |
    ISBN 9781772127553 (PDF)
Subjects: LCGFT: Poetry.
Classification: LCC PS8625.D6264 N67 2024 |
    DDC C811/.6—dc23

First edition, first printing, 2024.
First printed and bound in Canada by
Houghton Boston Printers, Saskatoon,
Saskatchewan.
Editing and proofreading by
Jannie Edwards.

A volume in the Robert Kroetsch Series.

University of Alberta Press gratefully
acknowledges the support received for its
publishing program from the Government
of Canada, the Canada Council for the Arts,
and the Government of Alberta through the
Alberta Media Fund.

Canada   Canada Council   Conseil des Arts
          for the Arts   du Canada

Alberta
Government

CONTENTS

4.

FIRST THINGS

This doesn't have to go in order;
that's the first thing.
I looked inside
an egg,
poked and blown
pristine, made clean

by the passing of its own slime. Inside
was a cathedral, upturned chalice, clean
as my own eye. A hole is a thing
to gather light. The sun's blown
its particles apart in order
to glow through this one, dead egg.

This doesn't have to go in order.
Crack, then slime; or slime first, then the egg
whole in your hand. Blown
glass. A trinket, a gift, a thing
easily given. Riddle wrapped up inside,
cased, laid, brooded, clucked upon, clean

as a whistle. An egg's
a thing
with feathers, but, order
of operations applies — a flashlight shone clean
through the inside
illuminates outline, diagram, edges blown:

a real chicken nugget, down over bone, clean
tucked tail and rolled. Egg
over easy, it looks easy. Asleep. Unblown.
No peep nor crack. First things
first. All in order.
Round inside.

I once saw a bird born inside
out. Heart pumping on down chest. A thing
that lived in egg,
but once born, died. Thrown and blown
away. To the white bowl of the sink I went to clean
my hands after. Last things follow first: Hygiene. Order.

ROADSIDE WILDFLOWERS OF THE NORTHWEST

1.
I don't know the names of any
flowers except the most obvious
ones — dandelion, strawberry, wild
rose — the ones whose forms sit flush
against the names — the strawberry
bears, the rose holds hips
and thorns.

2.
So this one morning I was down
at the bus stop and there was this young
woman talking to an older woman
who was clearly not too familiar
with the whole system of public transit.
"Which way does the bus come?" she asked,
and, having had it pointed, "Well,
when the bus comes around the corner,
how will we know it's the bus?
Will it have a sign on it that says,
BUS?" The bus came around the corner.
"Oh! It's a bus!"

3.
Buttercups I know. Forget-me-not
I can remember. I used to sit
on the front step eating chamomile
raw between the nails of my thumb
and first finger. I used to know
the names of my fingers in Swedish,
my aunt reciting, "Tummatott,"
that's one. Långeman. Lille vicke Dawn.

Fireweed is edible and best before
the bloom. Pigweed, a sort of spinach.
Kinnikinnick, we called it
honeysuckle. There's something else called
honeysuckle. We'd call it what
we want.

4.
Of course, there's a man in the story.
I met him on a hot day.
He's the kind of man that you'd know
the day you met.
"Stand in love, don't fall in love,"
he told me, but by then I was already lying
down.

11 CONVERSATIONS

1.
your neighbour was jealous of your lobelia
but you didn't know you had a garden

2.
I found a spider on a leaf and you found another one;
I said, perhaps they have some kind of relationship

3.
I called all my goldfish Nicolas Bourbaki
but you didn't think fish needed names

4.
tongue huddled in the corner of my mouth as
soundless as the tongues of paper clips. just holding

5.
I said there was a lacuna in your argument;
you said it sounded like a butterfly

6.
I'm sorry I accidentally used the Kali Yuga laundry cycle;
I guess it shredded our clothes and beat them with skulls,
but look — this one pair of pants came out Versace

7.
your voice against my sternum:
your voice was my voice

8.
hush, you said. you shouldn't
say those things. mmhmm, I said. mmhmm

9.
o—
—o

10.
the window
closes the door
from across the room

11.
only the rain is still talking to these trees

5 WAYS OF SHUTTING UP

1.
Do you like our sexual dimorphism, I ask.
He likes the way I fit into his armpit.
Inside the pit of the peach is a soft thing, and bitter.
A tongue out of the mouth.

2.
Loose lips sink ships.
Sunk ships drip drops.
Dropped drips plink plonk.
Plonked plinks clog sinks.

3.
Deep morning is a velvet box
and I a dull jewel, snug within.
The lid is prised up from the horizon.
Some hand will wear this ring.

4.
Like a telescope.
Like a lawn chair.
Like a freezerdoor.
Like a coffintop.
Like a conibear.

5.
Gulped down a gumball
from the 25c machine.
Kids say if you eat one it'll
swell in your guts and kill you.
You're gonna die
kid.

LITTLEST

it's the little things, modular
arithmetic, breathing — being
able to fix a hole
when your elbow's gone poky.
having a hand
in how your hand moves.
      I can ride a horse, I said, fire
      a colt. I used to be able to stand
      on my head but that's got wobbly.
      I can do an integration by parts.
      I can knit my own clothes. I can wear them.
      tryna big myself up.
they told me my toenails
are smaller than the average and also I have
tiny teeth. those little things. how small
I was beneath you, how your hand
engulfed. and how I turned
inside, and how we so quickly come
      to the part where I should, no doubt,
      discuss your sudden death —
your pale leaning death in the doorway languishing
your bright leaping death on the highway savaging
      but of course we just lost touch
      and I still wish you bits of the best
a deck of that wheat beer
a bed bought retail
a small thing.
      it was the smallest thing.
      love.

THE 2ND SHORTEST DAY

The brain bobbles on its stem, cold and sly.

Truck backs into the parking barrier, thunk chunk.

The bus is running 7 minutes late (23%).

This lowest layer of snow won't come off the sidewalk. It's unshovelable.

We loved each other before we did. We both know that.

Someone's kid stomps squealing into the flock of waxwings strewn like seed outside the store. "There were 42. I counted."

This gif shows how to wrap a present on the diagonal. Gasp magic.

The sun shivers at the mountain's tip, gets ready to roll.

We never thought we'd stop the stars when we put up all these satellites and shit.

Someone's cat triggers a light. We're holding hands. I can't see.

THE FAILURE OF WINTER'S FIVE-YEAR PLAN

Snow is a struggle,
one doesn't really know what for —
one of those dumbass
revolutions that doesn't last, somehow —
a real fast interregnum and then it's back
to grass, to all that bullshit about
flowers.

Snow gave it a shot,
you gotta give it that.

A child shaped it as a man.

There it squatted, legless, ran the lawn
with iron hand (specifically, a fork)
and shrank by days til, puddling,
it lumped to non-. Til the first
worm popped and chawed its maw
in the space that was the belly
of the storm.

QUICKNESS

"Did you ever hold a frog in your cupped
closed hands?" she asks. "It's like
that, only, you know,
right on top of your bladder."

the frog was rot-coloured,
leaf-veined. a splot
of bonefat, a wriggling towelette.
to hold was
shock, thrill, contact,
other, murder. trying not
to murder. to be so gentle
a trap. a house. an observation
tower.

"From here you could see," I said,
"so far. If I let you
out."

you kick.

I
like frogs.
I like the way

) when I opened (

it jumped.

INCREASE

children are like fungus —
alive, that's something
you can say about them.

growth is its own
value proposition.
love's supposed
to be automatic
like transmission.

children get bigger when it rains,
get bigger when it's hot,
get bigger through drought.
children follow the cube-square law:
their hearts slow as they grow.

children are like mice. they learn
to avoid the peanut-butter traps,
and drive you from your home.
you're downtown saying,
"I thought they were cute
at first. I can't
go back."

a child is a step toward a corpse,
and a step away.
the dead wall us in our siege city.
we see more birds than ever.
a bird is a symbol and a speck.
overhead, the moon, a bone egg.
overhead, the moon, a bone pushed through
a blackened skin.

children are fossils — past
dug up and cast in new
exhibits, to be seen and read
on the accompanying card.

children are paper clips
made of gray goo, a WHILE loop
that's true by definition.

children are on the ground,
in the yard,
under the house,
over the fence. love's supposed
to get lost while one counts
to ten, and make it easy
to be found. love's supposed
to grow like children do. to come
in when the streetlights go. to
live in bodies out of bodies

automatic. spreading. eating.
in the walls. according to rules.
its own reaction.

a child is a step.
a step is an operation.
a move, a cut,
a cup, a trip,
an embarkation. a state.
"I just love children,"
says everyone. I just
love. contamination.
out of the cut, fluid.

a child is
a fatal fungus.
that's
something.

APERTURE

I was looking for the fox
to snap and text to
you, your new phone.
Nature though was keeping quiet.
Nature was out of town.

Next morning I'll confess I overmarmaladed
the toast on purpose, trying to make up
for the chromatic deficiency, for orangelessness,
though the sky begins to show at times
we can observe, now, look —

the fox's tail flicks
from cloud to cloud.

A STRANGE REQUEST

"I collect rocks
from around the world,"
she said, "so bring
me a rock
from your garden."

She collects rocks
from around the world.

There's a rock
in my parking lot
kicked up against
the wall.

She has rocks
from around the world
and wants one
from my garden.

There's a rock by the door
to hold the door open against
the advice of management.
There's a rock in a can
where cigarette butts go,
and there's cigarette butts
everywhere that isn't in the can.

I stood by the door
and lit that one last cigarette
to smoke walking
somewhere else.
There was rain and I
hunched around my hand.

She wants my garden.
I have a rock.
She can't have it.

CHANGELINGS

1.
Her feet scare birds.
Such egglike
opening of the close-toed shoe,
such fluttering emergence.
Eeee. Gulls flock
and scatter. Cannot keep
to formation, gliding
downdraft on a path
that intersects the lawn.
She steps small on
the squidged-up wings she uses for toes.
Like running on
air, a useless
appendage made to serve. She likes
men with short arms. All
sorts of animals. And the shucked
sweaters of young children, long beyond
fitting. She likes
kicking up as she falls.

2.
Some pains hurts and others holps
distract from ones in tension
one and one makes anyone:
to win's her own invention.

3.

A car interior

        layered in dog

hair serves

        as a moveable

fur teacup.

        She, driver,

yells

        to sit. Yells

for speed.

        Drinks

from cardboard.

        Her slacks

need a lint

        brush. Her brew

cools. She's going

        and going.

Places

        aren't where she's at.

Her cup

        contains her.

THE FUNGUS SPEAKS

In some heads a mushroom grows,
   this layered thing,
      cap
      scalp
      cap.
Grey-pork gills exuding
spores and sweetness.

It has a delicate and nutty savour,
as of moss, evening and the twice-
bitten tongue. A blood champagne.
And the voices from late-night
television, imitation silk.

The fungus speaks.
[script]:

    they want you.
    they hate you.
    your rights. and fear.

    and now.

    and now.

In some sweet heads a mushroom grows:

It has rained all this August:

seeding into stalk, morel,
a victory broken off in the hand.

The ones with the all-meat heads
watch them. The all-meat heads
shake gently. It may become
necessary to involve authorities,
and if necessary, the all-meat
testimony will direct the outcome.

The weekly squeal gets the geese,
they say, and nod,
wise   and wide
and well informed.

And who is meat, and for how long?

In a place where many have a place.

In a world of increasing precipitation.

Where stem is stigma.
Where stigma is dissolving.
Where contact is contamination.
Where fluid is suspect.
Where hope is where the harm is.
Where no one's who he thought she was.
Where change is management.
Where management is leadership.
Where lead is flint.
Where mind is over and matter,
matter is a fungus germinating in
the loose, black, tender ground.

ABOUT THE AUTHOR

About the author hangs
      a nimbus of expectation and defeat.

Lichens lick her
      brain, fingernails, and heels

encrusted in a callus like a shoe.
      She walks a lot

but cannot walk
      this algae off her

an offer too good
      to be, etc. The way the mingled

lives and lifeforms of
      "this world," "the world"

wrap round her. All about
      the author hangs enigma,

penumbra, she's shadowed on
      three sides

(time, space, and doubt).
      The author has a body

like and liking other bodies.
      It digests poorly.

An uneasy colony, it sinks
      into moss or bed. It issues windy

proclamations. It reads.
      It grants itself place. Place

falls about in infinite wealth,
      isotropic and un–

bounded.

The author has a number
      of points to make, and numbers them.

FIRE WATER ASBESTOS MOLD

1. I've got opinions and
   you've got opinions so
   let's do a little remediation (sha la la)

2. tongues of flame gonna gobble
   up your g-damned marshmallows before you ever
   got a lick in

3. to remediate: first, wet an inconspicuous
   area of desired surface. surface,
   sink, penetrate, possess.

4. as best as I know that's about
   how it's gonna do. this right here
   is the hook, okay

5. hyphae produce spores. spores grow
   indoors and outdoors. all like it
   ain't no thing (sing it)

BIRD'S TEN

1. I am singing. Listen.

2. A sound is a wave that crashes, dissipates, folds in on itself.

3. My song is my own.

4. A bird sings in spring. A bird sings spring. Spring sings into a bird.
   Spring sings a bird into being, and a bird sings spring into being.

5. A bird is.

6. A bird isn't, then. But that's then. And later.

7. There is more than one bird.

8. When two birds sing the same song, they're the same bird.

9. Our song is our own.

10. The egg came first, but the egg could not speak its way open.

BINARIES (1)

two eagles crossed paths
                    at two different times on the same day

the path was in my eye
and in theory sky

anything up in the sky without scale
looks to be one size
                    and that one size is
about the size of a soup
bowl

hope you're hungry.
that's a fuck of a lot of

        moonsoup

        spiritsoup

an eagle's like a dog flying around up there.
medium sized out of the range of all *possible*
things, animals, things that a mind fits.

things conceivable

                    and having conception.

two eagles: one bald, one golden.

one has seen better days. two eyes.

and out of this eye, a glimpse of horizon.

and out of that eye, the wingtip of night.

BINARIES (2)

Yes, I know —
I put out two tendrils,
feelers on either side,
and made myself a wishbone,
waiting (eager) to be snapped.
Who'll choose for me

among binaries? Bend
me to prove my bent.
You know I started wearing
these antennae mainly to be different
in the most accepted alien way.
I think it was a costume bought

at the Dollar Store on November
1st because if you get far enough
behind that's like planning
ahead! (Wheels within wheels).
I started wearing the headband
with the springs and the googleyes

to get a better view
of space
(left) and time (right).
Or maybe
it was science and art.
I think I was also dating two guys.

One of them may not have known
we were dating. It was
a confusing time, is what I'm
saying. On the one hand,
a hand. On the other hand,
a fingerless glove.

They started letting us turn
right on red which contributed
to going in circles. In some
cases circles are squares. That's
topology. I kept trying to shape
my aura. It seemed like

diffusion wasn't good enough.
It was one of those Moments
when everybody has to Choose,
and they keep saying Time Travel
Isn't an Option. History
is watching with googleyes.

I shaped my aura into feelers.
I pulled on my pigtails to get them
tighter. I literally do not
know what the left hand
is doing. Amiright?

THE KINGFISHER

1.

wot's a kingfisher,
    precious,
just a bird with a great name
a flopamop with a marketing
    department

2.

we have sandpipers. robins (*Turdus migratorius*). the chipping
sparrow. wilson's warbler. hoary
(or common) redpoll (these are
easily confused. but anyone'd
rather see the hoary.) we have
birds. the eagle. the raven. the bank
and cliff swallows. the chickadee
deedeedeedeedeedeedeedeedeedeedee

3.

a year ago we didn't know the names to our own birds, my husband
(named Husband) and I (named I). we bought *Audubons*. we bought
Petersons. I acquired a 1936 *American Birds*. I gained access to a
comprehensive database called *Birds of the World*. some birds migrate.
some birds stay. some birds tell you what time it is. others what month
(with climate-altered slippage). some birds are out of their recorded
range. migration may be, just, each bird trying to get a little elbow
room from its fellow birds, taken to its logical conclusion. there's a
similar drift-and-pull in political opinion (not among birds). the
study of birds conduces to analogy. the amateur birdwatcher may be
distinguished by his eccentricity of dress and his unconstrained
attitudes. the expert wears earth tones and blends into the printed
page. the amateur knows not the names of things and calls them all,
"hey, you." only the owl responds to this gambit.

4.
the kingfisher is
  a poem.

the bird is a fluttering leaf among leaves.

the kingfisher does not come into these parts.

WALKING THE LONG LOOP

The wind shook my shirt like a salad spinner and I
laughed to see the stick stuck
high up the spindle-branched sapling, wondering
if the latter had grown that way,
the former losing over decades (ground)
or gaining (an earlier elevation).

I'd been dead before
and dropped a lot of weight.
I'd been ghosted a time or two.
I'd hit my head and pretended it hadn't happened.
You were the dark room with no loud noises.
You were the dark, I'd
allowed.

One day the wind will have my heart, I guess,
flash fried and let fly from the jar of ash,
assuming such litter is permitted, and you're there
to flip that lid.
I could do worse than to lodge,
even the barest bonescrap, atop
a nodule of pine. Anything
with sap in it, a line
to the nearest star.

The wind shook my shirt like a salad spinner and I,
not yet evolved to vegetable,
laughed and turned back against the gust.

.

.

.

But then, in the turning:

.

.

.

This is too pat.
I don't have a message.
I don't know what the hell I'm talking about. I shouldn't be trying to
fake it with a neat one-liner, some dumb summing up. I should leave
it ragged. I should tear the page. I should rip it like that rip that's still
there, above my pelvis, if I stretch too hard or try to flaunt myself. I
should leave it open and the ooze coming out.

so here is the edge

——————— and, here is where I am roughly balanced ———————

ONLY GENIUS CAN SOLVE THIS PUZZLE

How many harps in harpsichord?
Depends if the h's are identical, and the r's.
When I say, "I love you," is that the same
as saying, "I love you"? Or "I love you"?
The sounds between the sounds are ours.
Puns are koans' country cousins.
A tiny breath disrupts the dust,
makes jump just these few fond particles.
Brownian bumper cars.
It doesn't take much.
The breath that says, "anything,
anything at all."

TRANSCRIBED ON LEAVES AND THROWN INTO THE WIND

Sometimes I talk too fast and

.

.

.

[five lines missing]

.

.

... put my tongue in sprints.

The following is as follows:
one, a principle;
two, an eight on the Beaufort scale;
three, multiply by five to get the distance to the storm.

.

.

[approximately two-and-a-half
lines missing]

.

(full?) throat.

A BORING POEM

I'm so not interested in writing
any Northern/Nature/Yukoner poems about the Northern Lights and
my trusty-sled-dog-see-your-breath-adventure but all my poems turn
out to have animals in them because that's where I'm

and I do share 50% of my DNA with a banana

so I don't want to hear any more about how I'm
bad at sharing just because I'm an only child
and everybody's bad at assumptions

well at the end of the day I was born
here at the end of the day in a thunder
storm of anesthesia and incubation

an animal purred into that room, nipped
a neat umbilical, wolfed
my head right out the womb.   that's its breath

on the window page

    blurring

                it makes a real hot meat view

3.

LATELY WE'VE BEEN TALKING more about how Northern art is mostly in-migrant art, or art that's recognizable to Southerners who can imagine themselves migrating North — wow that's so *real*, those Northern Lights sure do resonate on a hipster wavelength — and how these folks just suck up the frozen air and push us into the snowbank shouting their glee over seeing mountains for the first time. The in-migrants: mostly White, mostly city. Mostly seekers. Prospecting for personal growth. Staking claims.

And yes, I in my turn (it's my turn) shove and elbow and shout my yawps over top of the voices of the fourteen First Nations and the eight First Nations languages, which voices anybody only wants to hear if they say the things we want to hear, e.g. the purging castigation and the mythic union and the sweet-sweet plunge through geologic time. And I am sorry. And I swallow. And I shout, "It's my time."

It's my time. Time runs up from the lightning storm over the hospital on the banks of the Yukon River and the cloth diapers drying on the line outside the cabin twenty minutes from the laundry-industrial complex, and time has always felt a thin thread to me, single ply and snappable.

I am speaking.

Words in time jumble and rearrange.

I have to sieve my words through the words of the quaint Northern folk song, the one that gets the grants and plays on CBC. Excuse me if it all comes aurora out moose sometimes kayak fucked.

OUR 80s WAS IRON MAIDEN t-shirts on 8-year-olds. A kid with a mustache in the Grade 3 class. Kids getting shit on by the teacher for their Pelly English. FASD.

The teachers come up to do their two years and leave. Or do their 20 years and drink. Is this what you were hoping to see on your trip?

WE ARE TASKED TO SPEAK TRUTH to the arbiters of truth, and to power our personal devices at the ubiquitous grid.

On the radio they were saying how technology is everywhere nowadays. We looked from the radio, to the lightbulb, back to the radio, which was about all we'd got.

> *Have you considered that someone coming in from Outside may know more than you? May I tell you (as I do) what to do? Have you considered your mid- to low-level employment as a natural consequence of your parochialism? You're a very natural person. That's your nature so we expect good nature and don't neglect to keep a naloxone kit handy in the event that your nature overwhelms you down by the riverbank or on the way to the office.*

Someone passed out in the hallway and was very embarrassed about it. That's natural. Self-effacement is simplest when face down.

But the missing and the dead have unique needs. Diversity must include those whose identity is absence.

PLEASE LEAVE ON

In 1989 at 3 p.m.
the teachers all wrote P.L.O.
in the chalkboard's corners
and we said, "That means
Palestine Liberation Organization,"
because we knew so much.

Our wisdom was the kind
that's learned in Current Events.
Current Events was the first five
minutes of Social Studies
class and the Social Studies
teacher was known to be dating a student.
We all said, "That's gross."

We got in trouble for looking
out the window and for reading
unassigned texts. We said
"You'll get the strap," and
"Nuh, they outlawed corporal
punishment," and "I heard one kid
still got it."

We got seated separately
from our friends and found ways
to exchange notes. The sky
was so full of ice, it fell apart.
We lost heat from our heads.
We knew several facts, and whether
to repeat them. They had us set
for life.

THE FORTS

The personal is heretical.
The political is inedible.
A Host is a dead person.
A ghost is a dead person with gusto.
A ghost is an ideology.
An owl is proportional.
Starlight is fairly distributed.
A nightlight is political.
A house is a diplomatic pouch.
A mouse is immunology.

Fist, section, fur, fort.
Count to five,
turn out, live.

GUN ETIQUETTE

The rifle is always loaded, and
to point is beyond impertinence.

The kids all smoke and say
"just joke." Our mouths

do magic with air and fireball,
sucked from the neck

hand-to-hand. Always prove
the barrel — a trapper down

in Watson left his standing
by the stove, then out

in the cold it iced and stopped
the charge in his face.

Our faces do tricks with smirks
and cancer sticks. We build

our houses of available materials.
One puff blows you sideways

but that's because you're drunk.
Never load unless you plan

to shoot. That's safety. Us kids
should know.

CHARTS

— fox troops the tracks —
— what would be his sign? —
— are animals born under houses? —

who has a thought to give for love,
would trade a calcium channel
for a bit of soft bread across your tongue?
for the tongue? for the ball
of your thumb?

night struggles home dragging
its blanket over its head and sighing
for the sympathy of the field mice,
to try to get a little kindness out of
the odd ant or grub. out of things
that root and skitter and, as a rule, do not
harbour the hot hope of dark
or pat its head or abjure
it to be okay. we all want what
we need from the one who can't.

this time of year our boots lack purchase
and we fail to grip the ground.
feet fly, arms flail.
we are born into houses and we home
to the handmade as down a compass-slope
slides the pigeon, the tern, those
magnet-minded. we want to know
what a month will hold.
in the newspaper. in twelfths.
in our pants pockets. in a fold
of dough. in writing, this time.

APOLOGIES TO A MOUSE

I have lived in harmony with spiders, silverfish.
        I looked you up on the Internet, little sisters,
        and Google said it was safe
        for us to live together.

Occasionally I did become tyrannical and vacuum you
        but then I felt badly. It was safe for us
        to live together so long as I
        could exercise restraint.

Mammals find these things more difficult.
        We need to buy a mousetrap, says my husband.
        There is poo on everything, our gear, our food.
        We could live in harmony, mouse, if you
        were not profligate with your poo.

Best to do it while it's still cold. It's pushing
        minus thirty. The light is lovely now,
        that ice-light. We'll have a lot
        of cleaning up to do.

— The bird is dead. The cat
is bored. Bored bored bored bored.

— The mouse is a bird. The mouse
is dead. It flew.

— Valerian opens the astral
gates. Cats close them.

— Low-flying planes drop water
on fires set by the heat of their flight.

IN A SCRUB PINE

My friend would like to donate sperm
because it would be great
to have a lot of little hims
running around, he thinks,
even though he's tried
to kill himself three times —
it's the world he tries
to isolate and blot, turn it all out
like a light and him a night
bird, keen to fly.

                    Me, I've capped my line.
                    No need to proliferate or go for an extension

on these genes — I've given blood
and made arrangements for my organs, but
to share of what you have is one thing —
you'd plate for guests a broken Triscuit
and a few of those bad Dad's
Oatmeal if that's what you've got — to add
to the sum of that with more of the like is
another, and in my estimation, not
to be borne.

                    We saw a golden eagle by
                    the river, or

a baby bald, I don't know
my birds. The seagulls had it pinned
in a scrub pine, keeping up their calls to keep it
hunched. They circled and it sat,
harassed, or just

no mind to bother — the mind
of a bird is never mine
to know, and I must not
assume. A mindlike
substance, fluttered, slight.

My friend would like some hims that are not him.
The eagle tucks its head against its wing.

AT HIDDEN LAKES

The pain in our bones brings
the animals out. Now

our motions ease
into animal-time. Green branch

Vs the water; dives.
Brown eyes peer

between brown ears.
Tail slides

without a slap.
Shows us straight

where's home. No threat
from our grinding bones.

We still and hold.
My toe, his hip.

The knee that pops
like a tail slap

on a rain-ringed pond.
The wet is in

the air, the pool,
the skin and soon

the hollows of these bones.
We note the joints

and move them slow. The beaver
looks and lets us look. The bear

ambles unvexed
upslope.

THE TOWN FILLED UP with foxes. The foxes are from Toronto, used to hang around Yonge Street. They know more than the coyotes about how to fit the canid niche in the local ecoystem. Better-dressed, too.

Deer come up from Vancouver. Invasive species know how to make our land produce. It's called development. There's a government department to spend our transfer payments on getting more of that. Thank you thank you we'd been so thin here on the ground.

(coyote)

                                        (coyote)

        (coyote)

(coyote)

THERE'S A LOT I CAN'T TALK ABOUT here, a lot that isn't mine to tell. From my own life, where I'm inside someone else's story. From the lives of the North: the modern treaty citizen, the temporary foreign worker, the International student, the refugee. I'm just some White chick who grew up in this place.

But sit with me and say these names: Carcross/Tagish First Nation. Champagne and Aishihik First Nations. First Nation of Na-Cho Nyäk Dun. Kluane First Nation. Kwanlin Dün First Nation. Liard First Nation. Little Salmon Carmacks First Nation. Ross River Dena Council. Selkirk First Nation. Ta'an Kwäch'än Council. Teslin Tlingit Council. Tr'ondëk Hwëch'in. Vuntut Gwitchin First Nation. White River First Nation.

The names, the people, the governments, the waterways, the lifeways, the land.

LOOK AT HOW WE DIDN'T KNOW how to live because only Ontario possesses the secret of right life. Look how we lived. How we slept over and stayed out and went out with each other and let the stoners cast the stones they could lay hands on, behind the school between the forest and the garbage cans, and we laid on hands. We hangmanned it and guessed the wrong letters and it was more, or love. It was in our hands. We were all cheap gloves and frostbite. We were smokers. We learned typing because it was the future. We were hands-on learners. We went outside at lunch and stared into the dishpan sun like Vitamin D was the only thing between us and getting a job.

OCCUPATIONAL CLASSIFICATION SCHEMA:
former Yukon youth aged 35–54

000000 — dead

000100 — missing

100001 — in jail

100100 — insecure attachment to the labour market

200000 — enrolled in academic upgrading

200100 — mid-level clerical and technical positions

300000 — addictions peer counsellors

400101 — freelance pharmacists

501623 — NDP territorial party leader

EVERY YUKONER OWNS THE 1979 Encyclopedia Britannica.

Every Yukoner grew up drinking homebrew.

Every Yukoner has tried hitching the backyard chickens to the kicksled as a labour-saving mode of transportation.

Every Yukoner has died of a fentanyl overdose.

Every Yukoner sells ice to every other Yukoner.

Every Yukoner glows in the solar wind.

Every Yukoner votes for their best friend in the by-elections.

Every Yukoner knows how to build a shelter out of egg cartons, parkas, and tax dollars.

Every Yukoner drives a 1988 Oldsmobile.

Every Yukoner sleeps sweet at the wheel.

LONGGONE OUTHOUSE BLUES IN 14 LINES

The *Omni* magazines in the outhouse.
I used to think it didn't rain at night.
It rains in summer, and summer is full bright.
Tin roof rattles and shouts.
Reading myself onto Mars.
Ash down the hole.
A nest of wasps to kill.
It is what it is and it's ours.

I was never coming back.
No more
bare ass.
No more hick shack.
I used to leave an open door.
At dusk the forest flickers. Falling. Past.

THE BLOODSHOES

To pluck a chicken:
> Boil water.
> Add dish soap.
> Immerse dead chicken; let feathers loosen.
> Use electrical wire to wrap the feet and bind to a pole between
> two pines.
> The headless carcass hangs.
> Stand, and pull.
> The blood will drip.

The next day:
> Head off to school in those bloody shoes.

The next night:
> The bloodshoes talk to each other
> in click tongue, in squeaks.
> The shoes aren't good jumpers. The shoes
> show interest mainly in each other. This leads
> to trips and falls. They wake at dusk.
> Listen — on the porch, under the shelf —

The shoes:
> "We used to be alive. I was. You were. You were. I was. I was.
> You used to push out your chest, my love, and run."

UNREGULATED WASTE MANAGEMENT FACILITY

Listen, all kids love
    to play at the dump.

I have no sister, but
    the trash is flesh to me.

We all have normal dreams
    of empty roll-on deodorant.

I have no brother, yet
    I'm wearing cast-off shoes.

Kids like it. It's
    a chicken-bone graveyard.

Each one could be
    the finger-joint of the gone twin.

THE ONE TREE

The one tree's out in the field, half dead:
dead on the left as you drive up
and dead on the right
as you leave:

where we hayed in the heat:
but mostly I remember
the tree a black brush stroke
above snow, and how on misty days
when "someone took the mountains"
it bled through.

Do I have to remember something
I can still go see? We sold the field
and the tree. But selling isn't killing,
and it's been half-dead forty years,
I guess, and half
is still alive.

Any thought I had of living
there was just a thought; I hated a lot
about that house. The milk that froze against
the wall. Slump ceiling, a stain halo over
head. Double-plastic and dark, the stapled
window frame. And I would not
go back.

I didn't ever used to climb that tree;
it wasn't one to invite small feet
or host a primate's clambering.

It stood apart: whoever cleared that field chose
to leave it, respect or sense of the picturesque
or just got tired felling, I don't know, and pulling
stumps. Once you let something like that stand
it stands and you stand back,
seems best.

I didn't shove a twig into my pocket.
I didn't section bark to have for keeps.
I left that place.

The shadow's cast
and rests
across the path.

WASP SUMMER

Like us, the wasps made paper
   to package pain.

They hung their sting-centric
   disco ball from the roofline

of the outhouse. We tried
   to blend our lives:

our shit, their venom.
   We leveraged

a can of old spray paint in
   the rearguard action:

neon green wasps lumped
   the walls. Like us, wasps

stop moving if their respiratory
   systems are impaired.

These functions cross the phyla:
   respiration,

digestion, excretion, reproduction,
   habitat selection

and modification. The outhouse
   kept our shit away from home.

Some people have no manners
   and no sense, move in

on your shit, punish you
        for coming back and making

more. The wasp decor will likely not
        catch on. The paint is remnant

of that summer's war. Splotches are
        ugliness to us, death

to the other. We cannot live
        together. We put it on paper

and do not feel better. The sting
        connects us, haunch to haunch.

THIS ISN'T THE HOUSE.

This isn't the house I grew up in.
We're both set in our ways.
I've walked on trails that pass uncomfortably close to trees.
I've walked on trails that humans don't use.
I found the head of an animal with fur still on.
This isn't the house I grew up in.
We've both gone our own ways.
I spooked a grouse and set him running.
I found the house of an animal with fur still on.
I walked past the feathers of the caught grouse, tumbled.
She's gone to feed the fox.
This isn't the head I grew up in.
I walked past feathers, loose, and lasting after everything alive has left.

CHIT CHAT

I mean autoplagiarism is obvs the only possibility for any internally consistent integral individual

I mean how many times you tell that story?

gonna sue you at the dinner table gonna report you to the conversation board association committee where you can go with your "broad appeal"

I mean there's this grouse that runs through all my poems. struts. showing tail. how many times I tell that story, about my father, about "nature's packaged food." guess what mofo, all a y'all and us are "nature's packaged food." could eat you up.

anyway grouse keeps butting in where not especially called for. upsets the cup. "look look," says grouse. "look look. look look. look look. look look."

I'm not a story. I'm a I'm. I'm not even a self.

"THERE'S ONLY TWO STORIES," they say, "someone comes to town, and someone leaves town."

∴ ~~story~~ where
someone goes on living in their town or lives out of town.

There's no "fish in its natural habitat" story. There's no "man digs a hole, puts an outhouse on it, shits there for 15 years before needing to dig another hole" story. There's no story where we live.

Part of the trouble here is that we conflate at least two distinct definitions of "story": 1) plot, that which grips the soul, and 2) significance, that which the soul should grip. If there's no story we'd rather not hear.

> we all think "Story" and
> story: beginning and
> here is the good man, is here
> spirit, help her,
> and ending isn't a way
> we're mostly comfortable, want
> over, again, told
> from the top.
> we all think "and then." and then.
> as if
> you could know which bits
> to tell.
> tell to
> the little. the small inside.
> you say self. we all think
> "one time" and "a far away" and mean
> like now, like a curve or that bent
> spacetime or the metric
> that lets you come back by going,
> on around.
> of course we want this.
> and we all.
> we think.
> the and

ACKNOWLEDGEMENTS

These poems were written in and shaped by the lands and waterways of the traditional territories of Carcross/Tagish First Nation, Champagne and Aishihik First Nations, Kluane First Nation, Kwanlin Dün First Nation, and Ta'an Kwäch'än Council.

Some of the poems in this collection first appeared, sometimes in earlier forms, as follows:

"11 Conversations" and "Quickness," *the /tɛmz/ review*, Issue 17 (Fall/Winter 2021)

"5 Ways of Shutting Up," *PULP Literature*, Issue 35 (Summer 2022)

"Aperture," *Eunoia Review*, March 15 2020

"Apologies to a Mouse," *The Antigonish Review*, Issue 196 (Winter 2019)

"Charts," *Grain*, Issue 48.2 (Winter 2021)

"First Things," "ONLY GENIUS CAN SOLVE THIS PUZZLE," and "Roadside Wildflowers of the Northwest," *The Malahat Review*, Winter 2021

"The Fungus Speaks," *QWERTY*, Issue 46 (2023)

"At Hidden Lakes" (as "Sitting by the Kettle Lake Each Evening"), *The Fiddlehead*, No. 296, Summer Poetry 2023

"increase," *Strange Horizons*, February 7, 2022

"Littlest" (as "Eulogism"), *FOLIO*, Vol. 36, Issue 1 (2021)

"Please Leave On," *IHRAF Publishes Literary Magazine*, July 5, 2023

"This Isn't the house" and "Unregulated Waste Management Facility," *Understorey Magazine*, Issue 21 (2021)

"Transcribed on Leaves and Thrown into the Wind," *Unstamatic*, September 30, 2022

"Wasp Summer," *Literary Review of Canada*, July–August 2023

Thank you to Michelle Lobkowicz, Cathie Crooks, Alan Brownoff, Duncan Turner, and Elisia Snyder at the University of Alberta Press. I am deeply grateful to the anonymous reviewers and jurors who recommended this work for publication and whose feedback was instrumental in bringing the book towards its final form. Profound gratitude to Jannie Edwards for her attention to breath, space, clarity and productive ambiguity—your insights were essential to this work. Thank you to my parents, Diane Parenti and Rick Macdonald, for putting me in the situation that resulted in me being the person who would write this book. You've had a grand adventure, and lived life on your own terms! For the seeds of poetry found in our conversations and peregrinations, thank you to Kaurel, Jennifer, Owen, Ian, Hiedi, Jeff, Jack and Fred. Thank you to Cea Person for telling your story and spurring me to reconsider aspects of mine. Thanks and love always and beyond words to Sean Pond and to Ellie Pond.